THE MAYBERRY MIRAGE

A Veteran's Truth

Brooke Leighanne White

Dedication

For the used, the forgotten, and the fallen; May their
silence speak through us.

Preface

This book is the recount of the Vietnam War, and its repercussions told in two voices. The main chapters are written in the first person, as though spoken by my grandfather, a Vietnam veteran. However, the words are mine. He has chosen to remain anonymous, but he entrusted me with his memories, his reflections, and the truths he carried in silence for decades.

The Foreword and the Epilogue are written in my own voice, as his granddaughter. They frame his testimony with the perspective of a later generation. A generation shaped not by combat, but by the silence the war left behind.

This choice of structure is deliberate. War never belongs to one person, or even to one generation. War becomes an inheritance, passed down in unspoken ways. What my grandfather lived, my mother absorbed. What my mother absorbed, I carried. This book is both his story and mine; bound together by the silence that ran through us all.

Acknowledgments

To Pa, for trusting me with your story. For encouraging me to write, create art, and to always do what I believe is best.

To Asha, who has helped me find the language for wounds passed down through generations, and who has held space for me to observe, accept and transcend legacy wounds.

To John, for supporting me in all that I am and all that I do; Your steady presence made these pages possible.

To Ross, and the many others who underwent name and identity changes as soldiers.

To Mom, without you, this book would not have been written. Thank you for breaking the pattern of inherited silence by allowing my voice to be heard and expressed, even when angry. Thank you for choosing not to pass the silence on to me even before you were able to break it for yourself. You taught me the power and importance of speaking my own truth.

To dad, whose laugh instantly filled the entire room with joy, and who taught me that the only thing I can truly control is myself. I choose to carry you with me as a guiding voice within my heart.

Table of Contents:

Introduction

I want to start by stating that this story of the Vietnam Era has affected multiple generations. I am the grandchild of a Vietnam Veteran, and although I am two generations removed from the war, I, too, have carried it on my shoulders. It takes more than one generation to heal deep-seated trauma. Certain events and the patterns of behavior and psychology they create are passed down as "legacy wounds." Unfortunately, legacy wounds often cannot be fully untangled without the effort of multiple generations willing to rewrite the story.

When my grandfather went into the Vietnam War, he carried a much different story than he does today at seventy-five years old. Back then, he believed he was doing his country, town, and family a great service by being loyal, by standing up when asked, and by becoming an adult ahead of his time. He moved his way up through the ranks, starting with the draft and ending as a drill sergeant.

The way my mother raised me was heavily influenced by her upbringing as the child of a drill sergeant. I am the first generation just far enough removed from the war to break the generational patterns it created, and yet I carry its weight.

I remember being 18 or 19 years old and believing that the thing that best represented my grandfather was his draft number, 55. I believed the war had made him who he was and had left the deepest mark on his life. He didn't talk much about Vietnam with me, but I could feel the impact it had on him in the way he carried his energy. I could intuitively see beyond the quiet exterior he presented to the world. That same year, I saw how quickly his anger could surface; something I had never really experienced with him before.

That summer when I was 18 or 19, my grandparents and I went on a cross-country trip in a motorhome. We started our journey in New York, and the Grand Canyon was our grand destination. Along the way, we arranged for my mother, younger half-brother, and stepdad to meet us in Las Vegas, where they would join us for the final leg of the trip to the Grand Canyon. We stayed in many KOA campgrounds as we traveled, but I wasn't allowed to sleep outside in my tent; I had to stay in the motor home. When my mom arrived, the same rule applied, but with her came more freedom and adventure in other forms. She took me out on the Las Vegas strip, where she gifted me the experience of getting a tattoo.

The tattoo began as a tribute to the trip and my grandparents, but within hours, it became a mistake. It was of a donkey; I thought it was a fitting symbol for my plan to ride one down the Grand Canyon. The donkey looked more like a pack mule. It wore a Mexican-style blanket with my grandfather's draft number on it, and on top of its head were purple glasses, just like the ones my grandmother was always misplacing (I would later learn her forgetfulness was due to

Alzheimer's). The tattoo was meant to honor them both, but it turned out awkward, imperfect, and permanent.

When we returned to the campsite, I showed my grandparents the tattoo. The tattoo triggered something deep inside my grandfather. He became infuriated, yelling at me, calling me immature. I was only 18 or 19, but this was the first time I had seen the anger that I had always sensed was waiting beneath his silence. At my age, he had already been forced into adulthood, but I didn't yet know any better. I didn't anticipate such a strong reaction when I chose the tattoo.

Experiencing that outburst, the residual anger of war redirected at me was traumatic. It became my first true exposure to Vietnam, the day I literally and metaphorically tattooed it on my shoulder and unconsciously chose to carry its weight. After that, I no longer wanted to be on the trip. I wanted to fly home with my mom as she had planned to do with my half-brother and stepdad, but she wouldn't let me. Instead, she followed the footsteps of her drill sergeant father and made me tough it out, just as she had been forced to as a child. She insisted I stay and make the long trip back to New York in the motor home.

The day after my grandfather unleashed those residual emotions, we continued to the Grand Canyon. The air in the motor home was thick, and no one enjoyed the sightseeing. We stopped briefly, took a few hollow family pictures for my mother, and left. Needless to say, I never did ride the donkey down into the canyon as I had planned.

You must know that today, at thirty-one, I have a great relationship with my grandfather. I share this story not to paint an ugly picture of him. I share this story to paint an ugly picture of war and to bring light to how trauma is carried forward through generations. We store issues in our tissues, and when emotions are left unresolved, they leak out in unhealthy ways.

As a young adult, my grandfather also gave me his war medals. By then, I already knew the story of how he had once thrown them away, how his mother had retrieved and kept them, and how they returned to him after her death. When he placed them in my hands, it felt like more than medals were being passed down. It felt like silence, grief, and history, bundled into metal and ribbon. I didn't want them. I wasn't ready to hold that kind of weight in my hands, but I couldn't bring myself to say no. So I stayed silent. In that silence, I realized just how easily war passes itself down; not just through anger or memory, but through the weight of what is left unsaid.

Today, I share with you my grandfather's perspective on how his generation was lied to and used by the United States Government. In some ways, this is me continuing to carry the war on my shoulders; however, it is also an opportunity to share my understanding of trauma and how it is sometimes passed down through generations. I hope this book will help readers to start carrying less weight on their own shoulders and, in turn, shift our society further towards love rather than ridicule.

The following pages will share my grandfather's perspective in the first-person narrative, though it is I who has written the words. He wishes to remain anonymous; Yet his heart aches to share his truth.

PART I: MAYBERRY

CHAPTER 1

The Mirage of Mayberry

I grew up in the kind of town that could've been the Mayberry depicted in the Andy Griffith Show. Front porches, handshakes that meant something, and neighbors who looked out for one another. It was the 1950s, and if you believed what you saw on television, life was good. *The Andy Griffith Show* turned small-town America into a kind of sacred image, depicting Sheriff Andy, his boy Opie, and quiet streets untouched by war, greed, or grief. That was the dream. That was what we were sold. And like most of us, I bought it.

My father owned a gas station. He wore a clean button-up shirt and worked long days. The smell of fuel and rubber hung in the air of my childhood, as familiar as the hum of the radio or the sound of customers calling Dad's name when they pulled in. There was dignity in that work, hard-earned and honest. In our world, that's what mattered. You didn't complain. You didn't ask for much. You did your part.

By the time I was seven, I had my own egg business. I gathered, sorted, and sold them to neighbors and local stores. Some mornings before school, I'd walk with my earnings to the grocery store and hand them over to the clerk to help pay down my mother's tab. That wasn't strange; it was just what you did when your family needed you. That's the kind of kid

Mayberry made, and that's the kind of kid the government wanted.

We were raised on loyalty. Every morning, hand over heart, we recited the Pledge of Allegiance. No questions. No hesitation. The rhythm of obedience was drilled into our minds before we even understood the words. In 1954, those words had been altered; "under God" was slipped in to distinguish America from godless communism. We thought it was an ancient tradition. It was actually Cold War propaganda dressed as patriotism.

Television sang the same song. *The Andy Griffith Show, Leave It to Beaver, Father Knows Best* all pointed to the same image; depicting that, America was good, authority was trustworthy, and everything would be fine if you just followed the rules.

No one talked about fear. Or trauma. Or the machinery working behind the scenes; government agencies tightening control, defense contractors lining pockets, military budgets swelling while families like mine scraped together grocery money. And we didn't ask questions. We had been trained not to.

CHAPTER 2

Born Into Obedience

I was always one of the smartest kids in the room and one of the most distracted. I'd ace the tests, but end up in the principal's office because I couldn't sit still or pretend to care about long division. Smart kids were supposed to behave. I didn't.

But even a restless kid like me couldn't escape the ritual that shaped us all: the Pledge of Allegiance. Every morning, like clockwork, voices rose in unison: "One nation, under God, indivisible..." Some loud, some mumbling, all the same rhythm. It was music. A chorus of obedience. The words stitched themselves into us long before we could question them.

At home, discipline came from my mother. She was fierce and proud, a woman who could silence a room with a look. She canned enough food each year to fill the basement shelves: beans, tomatoes, peaches. Each jar was more than food; each jar was a testament to endurance. She didn't just raise me; she raised my sickly cousin as her own, ferrying her in and out of hospitals, never once complaining. Sacrifice was the unspoken language of our household. You carried your share. You kept quiet. You endured.

The Church reinforced the message of obedience. God was not a metaphor in our home. He was a presence, authority, and comfort. Sundays moved the rhythm of the entire town. Sermons blurred the line between the Bible and the Constitution. Freedom was sacred. Sacrifice was holy. America was chosen.

When I was six or seven, I lay on my bed one afternoon, sunlight cutting across the room. And I saw Him. Jesus. Not a dream, not a feeling; I saw Him standing there, calm and kind. A presence so real I still carry it with me. That moment planted a compass inside me. Through the years, through jungles and nightmares, that quiet image returned.

So, when the draft letter came, it didn't feel like a choice. It felt inevitable. My childhood had been a funnel leading to war; from pledge, to pew, to sacrifice.

CHAPTER 3

Ghosts of the Depression and WWII

I never lived through the Great Depression, but I was raised by people who had. That shaped everything.

In our house, nothing was wasted. Bread crusts became breadcrumbs. Bacon grease went into a jar. Old grocery bags were folded like treasure. My father didn't trust banks. My mother stockpiled food like tomorrow might not come. We weren't poor, but we lived like we could lose everything any minute. The Depression taught them survival, but it left them with silence. You didn't talk about fear or weakness. You endured.

And just down the road from our home stood the church. The steeple bell set the pace of our lives, and Veterans of World War II filled our pews. They rarely spoke of what they saw in Normandy or the Pacific, but they didn't need to. Their silence was its own sermon. You nodded at them. You stood for the anthem. You didn't question their sacrifice. World War II became the measuring stick of manhood. If you could endure what they endured, you were worthy. If not, you were soft. That unspoken expectation hung over all of us. I grew up in the shadow of their silence. I didn't know then that the very values that made them endure hardship (obedience, frugality, loyalty) would be used to funnel my generation into Vietnam.

CHAPTER 4

A Nation on Edge

The 1960s didn't begin with peace and love. They began with fractures. In 1960, Kennedy faced Nixon. I was only ten, but I remember the debates weren't about policies; they were about religion. Could a Catholic be trusted to lead? Adults argued, prejudice dripping through every word. That's how I learned that bias could shape decisions as easily as reason.

Kennedy won by the slimmest margin. My family supported Nixon, clinging to conservative values. Kennedy's victory unsettled my family, but I remember wanting him to win. Within a year, he was tested by the Cuban Missile Crisis. Suddenly, nuclear war wasn't theoretical; it was on our black-and-white televisions. Schools ran civil-defense drills. We crouched under desks, arms over heads, as if plywood could protect us from firestorms. That fear burrowed deep.

Then on November 22, 1963, Kennedy was assassinated. I was in junior high when they dismissed us early, hallways echoing with confusion. At home, I watched the swearing-in of Lyndon B. Johnson, and within months, 40,000 soldiers were sent to Vietnam.

One of the soldiers sent was my uncle. He was twenty. I was fourteen. We were close, more like brothers than uncle and nephew. He sent home letters from Vietnam that were careful and vague. They talked about things like weather and food, but they were careful to speak of neither death nor fear. I remember noticing how his silence said more than his words.

The Mayberry dream unraveled in real time as the nation experienced civil unrest, prejudice, nuclear fear, assassination, and war. The promise of unity collapsed into silence and fracture. And soon, that fracture would swallow me, too.

CHAPTER 5
The Funnel of Indoctrination

Meanwhile, the media showed a sanitized version of what awaited us as soldiers. They showed helicopters, rice paddies, soldiers ducking for cover, but what they didn't show was the smell, the terror, and the silence that followed after someone took their last breath. The cameras came for pictures and left before the bullets. And then they went home and told our story for us. The first betrayal was being used like a weapon; the second was being misrepresented by the media.

By the time draft letters began arriving in mailboxes across the country, the funnel had already done its work. Boys raised in towns like mine believed we were answering a call. Only years later would many of us realize how carefully that call had been built around us.

When the draft letter finally arrived, it did not feel like the beginning of a story. It felt like the next chater in a story that had been forming for years.

PART II: VIETNAM

CHAPTER 6

From Boy to Weapon

Boot camp wasn't the beginning of my training; it was the final step in a process that had started long before I ever stepped onto the bus that brought me to camp.

By the time I stood in formation at basic training, head shaved, uniform stiff against my skin, rifle in my hands, it didn't feel new. It felt inevitable. Everything I had been taught, the pledge, the parades, the sermons, the silence of my parents, had been pointing me here. We didn't call it indoctrination. We called it patriotism.

In boot camp, that patriotism was stripped down and rebuilt into something sharper. Strangers in uniforms barked orders with voices loud enough to shake marrow. We weren't sons or students anymore. We weren't boys with futures. We were recruits being broken down, rebuilt, and pointed toward a target.

It was terrifying how natural it felt. When a drill sergeant shouted, you answered before you even thought. When they told you to run, you ran until your legs gave out. When they told you to fight, you fought the man next to you as if he were the enemy. The rituals of obedience we had absorbed as children became tools of the government. They smoothed away hesitation until reaction replaced thought.

Boot camp was where individuality died. They shaved your head so everyone looked the same. They took away your name and gave you a number. You kept your bunk tight enough to bounce a coin, your rifle clean enough to eat from. Discipline wasn't just demanded; it was survival. One mistake could cost more than a demerit. It could cost lives.

By the time we were finished, the transformation was complete. We had been turned into weapons, and weapons do not question their purpose. I told myself I was stepping into manhood, that I was proving myself. The truth was simpler, and uglier. The boy who once raised chickens and paid down his mother's grocery tab was gone. In his place stood a private in uniform, ready to fight a war he did not yet understand. And that was exactly what they wanted.

CHAPTER 7

Ambush Country

The jungle was alive in a way I had never known. It wasn't the soft green of the woods back home. It breathed like an animal; heavy, damp, filled with sounds that could turn from harmless to deadly in a heartbeat. You never really slept in the jungle. You dozed with one ear open, every rustle in the brush a question that tightened your grip on the rifle. Crickets, frogs, birds, the sounds blended until you couldn't tell what belonged to nature and what belonged to the enemy. Silence was worse. Silence meant the enemy was waiting.

We moved in single file, rifles at the ready, sweat stinging our eyes, leeches clinging to our legs. The air was so thick you felt like you were breathing water. The jungle demanded constant awareness. Awareness was not just observed with your eyes and ears, but awareness was also prevalent in the way the back of your neck prickled when something was wrong.

Ambush country, we called it. We called it Ambush Country because no matter how careful you were, the jungle always had the upper hand.

The first time I saw a man die, I felt two things at once: shock and inevitability. One second, he was whispering a joke to another soldier, trying to keep up. Next, he was gone. Training told me to keep moving, return fire, and stay alive; yet, every instinct told me to stop. To scream. Instead, I swallowed it down. By the third or fourth body, you didn't allow yourself to feel the same way. You couldn't. If you did, you wouldn't make it to the end of the patrol. That was how survival worked. Survival meant shutting up, turning off emotions, and keeping moving. The feelings didn't truly vanish. They hid. They waited. They came back later, in the quiet.

I remember one ambush in particular. A narrow trail, branches overhead twisted so tightly daylight barely touched the ground. I felt that prickle on my neck, but I kept moving. Then the world exploded. Gunfire, dirt, screams. My body hit the ground before my mind caught up. I tasted earth in my mouth. Time stretched into eternity. When it ended, the birds came back. The jungle returned to itself, but the silence was heavier. The trail was stained; we were fewer in troop size than when we started. That was the rhythm of Vietnam: sudden violence, then suffocating quiet. Life, death, silence, repeat.

CHAPTER 8

The Price of a Bronze Star

When the Army handed me the Bronze Star, they wanted me to believe it meant something. Proof of courage under fire, proof of heroism, but a medal can't tell the truth about war. The citation said I had shown gallantry. What it didn't say was that I was just trying to stay alive, firing where they told me, dragging a wounded man through the mud, keeping my body moving when every instinct screamed to stop. That wasn't gallantry. That was survival.

The men who didn't make it home never got medals. They got body bags, folded flags, their names carved into stone. Every time I looked at that medal, I thought of the faces not there to receive theirs. It didn't feel like honor. It felt like theft.

I dropped my medals in the trash. My mother found them. She didn't scold me. She didn't cry. She just picked them up and held them as if they were sacred. She kept them, not because she cared about recognition, but because, to her, they were proof I had survived. Proof that her son was alive.

Those medals belonged more to her than to me. She was the one who had lived the war every day I was gone; waiting at the mailbox, praying in silence, pretending life was normal while fear pressed down on her shoulders. If anyone earned it, she did.

Years later, I gave those medals away again. This time to my granddaughter. Not out of pride but because I couldn't carry them. When I gave them away the second time, I was met with stark silence, just as I had been practicing for years, believing that silence would protect me and others.

That's the reality of a Bronze Star; it doesn't represent courage, it represents survival. It represents silence. And the way that silence passes from soldier, to mother, to son, to granddaughter; heavy, unspoken, inherited.

The Army wanted symbols of victory. What it created instead were symbols of silence. Symbols of stories untold and memories that haunt soldiers in their sleep.

Medals suggest an ending, but for many of us, the war was only beginning its quiet journey home.

PART III: COMING HOME

CHAPTER 9

Coming Home to Nowhere

Coming home should have been the end of the story. For months in the jungle, that was the promise I held onto; the idea that *if I could just make it back, everything would feel safe again.* Yet, the moment I stepped off the plane, I knew that home wasn't the same. Or maybe home was the same, but I wasn't.

The first thing I noticed was the quiet. Not the silence of ambush country, but the silence of people who didn't know what to say. Neighbors waved, but their eyes slid away. Old friends struggled to talk to me, as if my uniform had turned me into someone they couldn't recognize.

At the gas station where I had once watched my father joke and shake hands, I now overheard mutters: *baby killer.* They didn't know me, but they thought they knew what Vietnam meant. They thought it was written all over me. I didn't argue. I didn't explain. I carried the weight the way I had been trained to, quietly.

At home, my mother tried to fold me back into normal with home-cooked meals, small talk, and chores, but when I sat at the table, I felt like a guest. Even family conversations grew brittle. They wanted me to be grateful to be home and alive. I was grateful, but I couldn't tell them what it felt like to wake in the night, reaching for a rifle that wasn't there. They wanted a son returned, but I was a soldier returned, and that was something else entirely.

Some men came home and threw themselves into work. Others drowned in alcohol. Many disappeared. We didn't have the language of PTSD then. Society had the words "shell shock" if people were kind and "crazy" if they weren't, but what we had most of all was silence. Silence that seeped into marriages, into fatherhood, into friendships that never quite recovered.

I walked down streets I had known since childhood and, I felt like a ghost. Home wasn't home anymore. Home became another battlefield; one where you fought to belong, to stay quiet, to survive the silence. The hardest truth was that you can't really come home from a war because part of you never leaves the jungle; the part that does come back doesn't know where it belongs.

CHAPTER 10
Trying to Rebuild Mayberry

Work was supposed to fix me and make me a part of Mayberry again. That's what we were taught: that if you keep your head down, work hard, and provide for your family, then the cracks will stay hidden. Maybe even heal. So I worked. Long hours, calloused hands, sweat that blurred the memories for a little while. Work didn't ask questions or care if you woke in the night with your heart pounding. Work only demanded that you show up, but no matter how many hours I put in, the ghosts were still there. Some days, they whispered. Some days, they screamed.

At home, I tried to play the role of husband and father. I wanted to be the man Mayberry promised: steady, strong, dependable, but war changes the way you love. It hardens where you should be soft. It makes you distant when you should be close. I carried silence into my marriage, into my children's lives. They felt the weight of something they couldn't name, the same way I had felt it in my father after the Depression and my neighbors after WWII. We didn't call it trauma. We called it being "a hard man." This was how the war continued living inside of us.

I followed the Mayberry dream; I bought the house, mowed the lawn, waved to the neighbors, and went to church. From the outside, it looked like the picture of small-town America, but on the inside, it felt fragile. Forced, like I was trying to build a house out of rotten boards.

The truth was, none of us could rebuild Mayberry because Mayberry had never been real. What we built instead was a generation haunted by what we couldn't say. Men worked themselves numb. Women carried the load at home. Children grew up with fathers who were present in body but absent in spirit. We thought silence would keep the war from spreading. Instead, silence became the way it spread.

CHAPTER 11
The Generation That Got Used

We were called the lucky ones. We came home. We worked. We raised families. However, beneath the surface, Vietnam kept taking its toll. Not on the battlefield anymore, but in hospital rooms, bar stools, divorce courts, and funeral homes. So many of us never really came back. Some drank themselves numb. Some carried jungle habits home in the form of pills or harder drugs. Too many ended their lives, deciding silence was heavier than death.

The war also followed us home in our bodies. Agent Orange, jungle rot, cancers that doctors denied for years. Our lungs, our skin, our blood carried the evidence of a war the government wanted to forget; our bodies refused to let it fade.

And it wasn't just us. It bled into our families. Wives carried households on their backs. Children inherited anger they didn't understand. Generations learned silence as an heirloom. Quick tempers, guarded hearts, distance where closeness should have been.

We were a generation that got used. Used for our bodies, for our loyalty, as examples of patriotism when convenient, and discarded when the country turned its back. When the cameras moved on, when the politicians wrote their speeches and tucked the war away into history books, we were still here. Carrying it. Quietly.

I often think of the boys whose names are etched into the Wall in Washington. I think of the men who came home broken and never found their footing. I think of the ones who mowed lawns and paid bills, but carried a hollow place inside that never healed. That's the legacy of Vietnam; not just battles fought overseas, but the generations scarred at home. We were told we were fighting for freedom. What we were really fighting for was profit, politics, and a lie called Mayberry.

The silence we believed was protecting our families was often the very thing that carried the war into the next generation.

PART IV: LEGACY & LESSONS

CHAPTER 12
The Lessons We Paid For

When I look back on Vietnam, I see more than my own story. I see the cost a nation chose to bury.

Nearly 58,000 Americans died in Vietnam, but the numbers don't tell the whole truth. By the early 1980s, studies showed that more Vietnam veterans had taken their own lives than had been killed in combat. That's how deep the silence ran. They called it PTSD eventually, but for years it was just "weakness" or "craziness." What we really had was an unspoken wound.

And then there was the poison. Agent Orange sprayed across jungles, clinging to our skin, staining our blood. Cancers, heart disease, and birth defects in our children. For decades, the government denied what we already knew. They left us to rot in waiting rooms while the war kept killing us, quietly.

The damage wasn't only physical. Divorce rates among Vietnam vets were sky-high. Alcoholism, drug abuse, and homelessness all spread like wildfire. By the late 1970s, one in four homeless men in America was a veteran, most of them from Vietnam.

We were told we had fought for freedom. In reality, many of us came back to fight for a roof over our heads, for recognition, for scraps of dignity. If there's one lesson I want the next generation to learn, it's this: patriotism without question is dangerous. We were raised to think obedience is loyalty, silence is strength, and sacrifice is endless. But governments can use those values against you. They can wrap greed and politics in the language of honor, and boys raised on Mayberry will line up to die for it.

I don't say this to shame service. I still believe in courage, in standing up for your community, in loyalty to your neighbor. But loyalty without truth is blindness. And blindness is what sends generations into wars they never asked for.

What are the lessons we paid for?

- Silence is not strength. It is surrender. Speak, even when your voice shakes.

- Patriotism is not obedience. It is a responsibility. Question the powerful.

- Sacrifice is not endless. Don't let anyone tell you your body, your mind, and your family are just "the cost of freedom" while they count their profits.

The Vietnam generation paid in blood, in silence, in broken homes and broken bodies.

If the next generation can learn from us, then maybe the price we paid won't have been for nothing.

CHAPTER 13
The Echo

For my generation, silence became a second language. We came home with medals we didn't ask for, memories we couldn't share, and wounds we couldn't name. We tried to bury it in work, in bottles, in marriages that strained under the weight. But silence doesn't stay buried. It leaks. It echoes.

The echo is how trauma survives beyond the battlefield. It's the quick temper that startles a child. It's the distance in a marriage. It's the guarded heart that can't say "I love you" without flinching. The echo is how wars repeat; not in jungles or deserts, but in kitchens, in schools, in the way families carry unspoken pain forward as a harsh reality. Over time, unaddressed trauma changes hands.

For me, the medals became part of the echo I am describing. I tried to throw them away. My mother pulled them from the trash and kept them, believing they meant survival. Later, I passed them on again, not because I wanted to, but because I couldn't carry them anymore. And now, my granddaughter carries the medals, and my story is etched into her skin as a tattoo.

The echo is not just about memory. It is about inheritance. The weight of war passed down in silence, in metal, in ink. What I want to make clear is that the echo doesn't have to continue.

We can break the echo. We break it by naming it. By speaking it. By refusing to let silence continue the war now that we are back home.

CHAPTER 14

Breaking the Silence

Wars don't end when the shooting stops. They echo. Through silence, through anger, through generations. Mayberry was never real, but the cost of believing in it was.

I was lied to. My generation was used. We carried that use like a badge of honor until it nearly destroyed us, yet although in smaller numbers, we are still here. We still have voices left. If we speak with them, maybe the next generation won't inherit our silence. The echo only continues if it's left unnamed. If there is one thing I want to leave behind, it is not medals or silence, it is truth. Truth that hurts, but heals. Truth that refuses to be buried. Silence is the soil where lies grow. Truth, even when it shakes your voice, is the only way to stop the echo. Today, maybe the echo can serve as a call. Not a call to obedience or silence but a call to honesty, to courage, to love, to speaking your truth. That to me would be true freedom.

Epilogue

I grew up in the shadow of my grandfather's silence. I didn't fight in Vietnam, but I carried it in the way he looked away when questions got too close, in the quick temper that flashed and faded, in the medals he tried to give away, and the weight I couldn't refuse. I bore it on my shoulder, inked into my skin, before I even understood what it meant.

For years, I thought the war defined only him. Draft number 55, drill sergeant, Bronze Star, survivor of ambush country. Now I've come to understand that the war didn't just define him, it shaped me too. His silence became part of my inheritance. His wounds became a part of my story.

That is what legacy wounds are: patterns of pain passed down like heirlooms, tucked into families and waiting to be named. My grandfather's silence became my mother's hardness, and my mother's hardness became my own questions unspoken. And now, as I write this, I understand that the choice is mine. The silence can stop here.

I tell his story not to paint him as a victim, but to honor his own personal truth. For decades, he carried what he was told not to speak and could not bear to speak. Now, through me, he has spoken. In speaking, something shifts; The echo softens.

The medals tell that story, too. My grandfather tried to discard them. His mother saved them. He gave them to me, and I carried them for a few years, but then, knowing their weight, I passed them on to my mother. They have moved from hand to hand, generation to generation, never just metal and ribbon, but carriers of silence, grief, and endurance. From them, I learned something vital: I can choose what physical, emotional, and mental things I carry.

Through writing this book, I realized I had more than one inheritance. On the other side of my family, my second grandfather stood at the edge of the same war. He was registered as a soldier, called to serve, and yet he chose a different path. He fled. He shed the name he had been given at birth and built another life, not in obedience but in resistance. Where one grandfather embodied discipline and silence, the other became a hippie, teaching me to take up space, to question, to resist the systems that demanded submission. Between them, I saw two versions of the same echo: one bound in silence, the other in defiance.

By healing through generational trauma and the echo passed down from both sides of the war (the hippies and the soldiers), I've also learned that I can choose how I perceive. The tattoo on my shoulder doesn't just mark my grandfather's past; it marks my choice to carry the truth with my voice and let go of the pattern of silence.

This book is not just about Vietnam. It is about every family that has carried war home with them. It is about every child who has felt the weight of anger that wasn't theirs, every grandchild who has asked why silence fills the room. It is about daring to break cycles, to remember differently, and to choose what legacy echoes forward.

References

John F. Kennedy Presidential Library and Museum. (1960, September 12).
Address to the Greater Houston Ministerial Association.

John F. Kennedy Presidential Library and Museum. (1962). The Cuban Missile Crisis, October 1962.

National Archives. (2016). Vietnam War U.S. military fatal casualty statistics.

Tanielian, T., & Jaycox, L. H. (Eds.). (2008). *Invisible wounds of war: Psychological and cognitive injuries, their consequences, and services to assist recovery.* RAND Corporation.

U.S. Army Center of Military History. (1983). *MACV: The joint command in the years of escalation, 1962–1967.* U.S. Government Printing Office.

Brooke Leighanne White is an author, educator, herbalist, and artist whose work explores the relationships between psychology, culture, environment, and healing. Raised in New York's Finger Lakes region and now living in Hawai'i, she draws inspiration from the landscapes, traditions, and stories that shape people's lives.

Brooke is fascinated by the ways people are shaped by family narratives, cultural belief systems, and the environments they inhabit. Her writing explores the relationship between identity, belonging, and meaning-making. Her writing draws from both personal experience and cultural narratives.

Brooke believes that healing is rarely one-size-fits-all and that people thrive when given the support they need to reconnect with their innate capacity for wellness. Sometimes that support comes through relationships, movement, herbalism, therapy, conventional medicine, or a combination of approaches. She is the founder of Sun-Kissed Botanicals, an herbal company dedicated to education and products that help people build meaningful relationships with the natural world.

Brooke encourages people to look beneath accepted narratives, reconnect with their own experiences, and cultivate a deeper understanding of themselves, their communities, and the world around them.

Learn more about Brooke's writing, herbal education, and products at:
www.sunkissedbotanicals.com